For Anishan - with love

Joseph

Retold by Felicity Henderson

Illustrations by
Toni Goffe

D0918718

A LION BOOK
Oxford · Batavia · Sydney

Long ago, in the land of Canaan, there lived a man called Jacob.

He had twelve sons. They all worked hard, looking after their father's sheep.

Benjamin was the youngest son. But of all his sons, Jacob loved Joseph best.

One day Jacob gave Joseph a beautiful coat. This made the other brothers jealous.

"We work harder than he does," they said. "Why should Joseph get all the best things? Why does our father love him more than us?"

One night Joseph dreamed that his family were sheaves of wheat in a field. His sheaf stood up straight while all the others bowed down to it.

His brothers were annoyed when he told them about the dream.

Later Joseph made his brothers even more angry.

"I had a dream last night," he said. "I dreamed that the sun and the moon and eleven stars bowed down to me."

"Be quiet!" replied his brothers. "We are not going to bow down to *you*."

Joseph's brothers got tired of his
dreams. And even his father told him
to keep quiet.

"That's enough, lad," he said sharply.
But secretly Jacob wondered about his
son. Although Joseph was boastful
and proud, could God have a special
job for him, when he was grown-up?

One day Jacob sent Joseph to find his brothers. They were far from home, looking after the sheep.

It was a long journey.

The brothers saw Joseph coming, wearing his special coat. Then they remembered that their father loved him most.

"Here comes the dreamer!" said one of them.

"The big-head!" said another.

Some of the brothers hated Joseph so much that they made a plan to get rid of him.

"I'm fed up with the way Father listens to him," said one. "Him and his fancy coat!"

At last Joseph arrived at his brothers'
camp. He had brought them some
lovely food from home and he wanted
to tell them all the news.

But, before he could open his mouth,
some of the brothers pulled off his
special coat and threw him into a deep
dry well.

They sat down to eat the food and
took no notice of his cries for help.

Just then the brothers saw some camels in the distance.

"Those traders are on their way to Egypt." said one. "Let's sell Joseph to them as a slave. They will take him far away and we can make some money."

So the brothers sold Joseph to the traders. They were going to the far-off country of Egypt.

It was a long journey and Joseph wondered what would happen to him there.

Meanwhile the brothers were up to more mischief. They had kept Joseph's coat and put some blood on it. Then they took it home and told their father a wild animal had killed him.

Jacob was very upset. "My poor boy!" he cried.

In Egypt Joseph became a slave to a very important man. Life was very different from when he had lived with his father and brothers. He wondered if he would ever see his family again.

Sometimes Joseph thought about all the things that had happened. Perhaps he had been too boastful about his dreams. He was sorry he had been so proud.

"I'm all alone," he said sadly. But then he remembered that God was with him and he felt less lonely.

Joseph decided that now he would work hard to please both God and his master in Egypt. If he met his family again, he wanted them to be proud of him.

Text copyright © 1991 Lion Publishing
Illustrations copyright © 1991 Toni Goffe

Published by
Lion Publishing plc
Sandy Lane West, Oxford, England
ISBN 0 7459 2125 6
Lion Publishing Corporation
1705 Hubbard Avenue, Batavia, Illinois 60510, USA
ISBN 0 7459 2125 6
Albatross Books Pty Ltd
PO Box 320, Sutherland, NSW 2232, Australia
ISBN 0 7324 0475 4

First edition 1991

Printed and bound in Singapore